GORILLA

Also by Christine Hamm:

Saints and Cannibals
The Transparent Dinner
Girl Into Fox
Echo Park

GORILLA

Christine Hamm

THE WORD WORKS
WASHINGTON, D.C.

THE WORD WORKS
P.O. Box 42164
Washington, D.C. 20015
editor@wordworksbooks.org

Cover art: Christine Hamm
Cover design: Susan Pearce
Author photograph: Christine Hamm

LCCN: 2021933188
ISBN: 978-1-944585-42-6

Acknowledgments

Some of the pieces titled "Gorilla" were published in *Apesh*t*,
     an anthology edited by Bill Oliver.
Some of the pieces titled "Latrines" were published in
     modified forms in a chapbook, *A is for Afterimage*, by
     the *New Orleans Review*.
"Changeling," "The Animal Gift," "Becoming Your Mother,"
     "Learning to Swim on Dry Land" were also published
     in *A is for Afterimage* in modified versions.
"What Happens When You Try to Write" was published by
     Everyday Genius.
"How to Make a Red Coat" was published by *Failbetter*.

Thanks so much to my husband, Dan, who puts up with my
hours of absence writing every day, and thanks to Joanna
Fuhrman, who has helped to give me the courage to write weird
things, and thanks to Jenny Xie, who convinced me to keep
sending out this manuscript, even after eight years, and thanks
to Nancy White, for being an amazing editor, and thanks to The
Word Works, for selecting this book as a winner, after so many
times as a finalist!

Contents

To Russell Edson, who first introduced me to the absurdist ape

Why don't you have the butcher cut these apes up? You lay the whole thing on the table every night; the same fractured skull, the same singed fur; like someone who died horribly. These aren't dinners, these are post-mortem dissections.

—"Ape" by Russell Edson

Gorilla

He says, *Gorilla, huh!* as if it were something with a mind of its own. The Gorilla is not real; the Gorilla is made out of rubber, synthetic hair and dark. The Gorilla has real action eyes. They blink up and down when you snap your head back and forth. The Gorilla tastes like Old Spice and hair cream on the inside, with a faint odor of Amstel and burning leather.

Safe Word

He was telling you about his toys. He listed things made out of metal and animal hide, things that used electricity and sparked occasionally, things that clicked and linked together. You said you weren't sure and he said he would go slow, so slow that you would forget to stop him once you began to feel pain. You said it was already hurting and you wanted him to stop. He said he stopped yesterday, that you forgot you were on a boat talking to him on the phone, and that he was still in New Jersey. You said that if he was in New Jersey, why were you still wearing a blindfold. He said you couldn't see because it was night, and that it was okay to go to sleep now, just close your eyes and let go.

The Moody Gorilla

The Gorilla dislikes rain and overcast skies—during this type of weather, you will most often find him on the toilet or shivering in a hidden nook under the tree.

Pet Cow

You only see her in summer; in the winter, some man comes, but not often. Short, sharp fur, scar near her shoulder in the shape of California. Black and white and black. Does not hesitate to shit on you when you get near her tail. Eyes like limpid balls of goo or something you could stick your thumbs into. Liquid dotted by vague filaments, possibly parasites. Some man with cold hands, fingers that feel very rough on her teats.

You used to tease your skin open with an X-Acto knife. Ear surrounded by dark swarms. Slow to look and poke, barely interested in what you have in the hand behind your back. She lets you lift her right front hoof and scrape between her toes with a hoofpick. Someone whose voice she never recognizes, no matter how often he calls. You used to tie the trussing string from the roast beef round your arm till your fingers turned dark. Nyquil hummed you to sleep at night, green buddy, thick mulch tongue. His hands, rough and cold. She's a summer animal: You imagine her visible barnbreath in winter, her huddling next to other cows through the dirty slats, one munching on her tail, on the tip of her tail till it bleeds like a nipple.

Gorilla

When you are left alone, you sneak into the Gorilla's bedroom and caress all his ties, their indigos, scarlets and maroons, their whites as blank and pure as an empty mask, their soft, soft silk on your cheek, like some sort of brilliant and nonviolent appendage. As long as you have known him, the Gorilla has complained about having to wear ties. Each Christmas, you give the Gorilla another one, sometimes two.

Changeling

In five languages, you are trying to learn the word for *orphan*. You think it's easier than telling the truth. You miss your Mother, although she was alcoholic and asthmatic and cheated on everyone she touched. Although she never wanted you, and would rather sing to her seals and fish, turning into a seagull and back under an overturned boat, humming about the saints and trains. In Polish, the word for *orphan* is the same as the word for *tin cup*. You believed that. You collected small wild things in a blue plastic bucket, showed them to your not-Mother. Your not-Mother shrieked like a cat with a stepped-on tail, demanded you dump them back in the forest. She quivered and laughed behind curtains. Could you help it if nothing had learned to run from you? Were you to blame if a garter snake, pure muscle wiggling, felt good on your palm, and even better on your tongue? You never learned the difference between your inside and outside voices. Your not-Mother made you sleep in the garage for three days. You pinched spiders from the rafters into a jar, and nestled with mice in the hood of your fur jacket. Your chin on the garage floor, you watched a flower unfurl over the driveway in the morning, then wrap itself away at night. You wanted to call it *orphan*, but your not-Mother told you, *that's incorrect*. You never found the name for this, its fine, electric-green vines, its pinkish face like an old ear trumpet, pointing at the sky to hear.

Gorilla

When the Gorilla feels something bite the skin under his shoulder blade where he can't reach, his fur ripples. It's actually a series of muscles contracting and releasing along his spine, but it looks like a breeze snaking up a hill.

The Rival

Your Mother gets a flying baby. She already has four cats and two dogs. When you come on Saturday, the baby is tied to a banister, flying up around the ceiling. *Mom, you need to keep that ceiling fan off,* you say. The baby smells funny, its diaper sagging and its skin loose. Orange and yellow hair grows all over its hands. *A baby is a lot of responsibility, Mom*, you say. You snap your fingers at the baby, trying to get it to fly down to you. The baby doesn't even look, just keeps fluttering its sticky wings and bumping into the walls. *It doesn't look right,* you say to Mom. *I feed it every day,* she says, *and spray it with water, they said that babies need a lot of water.* You ask your mom, *Where's its bottle?* She says, *Somewhere, somewhere.* She digs into the pile of soaking dirty dishes in the sink. She's wearing her t-shirt with the embroidered reindeer on motorcycles. *Why are you wearing that?* you say. *It's not even Halloween yet.* She feeds one of her toy poodles a soft blob from the sink. You hear the baby bump in the hall, its wings whirring like a blender. The baby makes a sound—something between a toy fire engine and a bark. *I think the baby's crying,* you say. *Oh, he will stop on his own,* your Mother says, *he always does.*

Music + Beer + Gorilla

Music + Gorilla

On Saturdays, the Gorilla likes to slide his favorite record, *Little Trees*, on the record player and lean back in his nubbly blue recliner and watch you through his eye holes. His favorite song goes: *Burn the little trees, yeah! Free the tiny bees, oh! Let the birds' wings singe, oh yeah!, oh, oh!*

+ Beer

You and your brother don't really know how to dance, so you stomp, sway and sometimes twirl. On the word *bees*, the Gorilla unleashes his leather belt. *Dance*, he says as he whips your calves. He is pretending to be another kind of Gorilla, the sort of Gorilla found in old movies with lots of eyeliner and a turban. This kind of Gorilla sits cross-legged and is fed grapes. *Dance*. This kind of Gorilla speaks with a heavy accent and has tons of nubile, hairless daughters who just wait for instructions, standing naked in a corner.

Disaster Porn

He rips the door off the hinges at 4 AM—it's not even locked. He stumbles and hits his head on the chair. He lies still, his mouth slightly open. You can smell the piss on his pants—there's a yellow trail of translucent vomit down one arm. His eyes are so swollen they look like leaking red fruits, as pulpy as plums. He makes himself a bowl of blackberry ice cream and falls asleep. He tips over, wakes up; he steps on the cat's tail, he steps on the cat. He leaves the refrigerator door open, knocks milk all over the red-tiled floor. He turns on the gas stove. He tries to light a cigarette and sets his beard on fire. Milk footprints follow him into the bathroom. He tries to make a knot of the shower curtain and hang himself, he tries to take off his shoes and pants at the same time. He ends up face down in the tub, scrabbling and slipping. He pauses: his breath is wet and heavy. After a moment, he asks for a beer.

Gorilla

Most mornings, you find the Gorilla quivering in the corner of your bedroom like a wild animal, his breath rasping and faltering. You pull the covers up over your arms and neck; you pretend not to notice.

Latrines

How you were still crying at the breakfast fire, around the burnt sausage in your mouth. Shaken cans of 7UP exploding on our t-shirts, hot dogs with stripes like prison pajamas. We sang in harmony with the record, sometimes you went a few notes higher for contrast. Peanuts made you go to the hospital, boys pretended to like you during recess and made you cry after school. How Billy, the counselor with the scarred lip, told you his dad did it. How you hated your white fat face. You kept saying that, *I hate my fat face*, when we'd look in bathroom mirrors. Almost matching floor length blue dresses, with transparent flowered sleeves, for the graduation song. Holding hands during the song, the sun so strong I closed my eyes. As you got hot, you smelled more and more of lemon and old tires.

Your Version of Swerving

After "Traveling Through the Dark" by William Stafford

On your street: no street lights, couples making out in darkened cars, and animals always getting hit. Once you and your family were walking George and you saw a deer lying by the side of the road, an almost dead deer, its hind hooves still shaking, its eyes staring, fixed. Your brother picked up a pine branch and poked the deer in the belly. The deer made a small *Uh* sound. *Don't*, your Mother said, *it has germs on it*. You went to your brother and took the stick. You poked the deer in the chest twice. The deer remained quiet. *Don't*, your Mother said, *that's disgusting*. George walked over to the deer and started licking the blood at the deer's mouth. *George!* your Mother said. She hauled on his collar. *George!* your brother said and pushed him with his toe. You said, *George*, and poked at the deer's eye. The morning quivered. George made a noise deep inside, like soft cloth ripping.

The Gorilla's Equipment

A catcher's mitt. A Country Cruiser with stick-on wood grain. Black wing tip shoes, polished once a week. A pile of banana leaves. An ancient leather belt, cracked along the buckle holes. Five brown glass bottles, full of Amstel. A stick, for poking at anthills, then licking the ants off of. A poor falsetto singing voice. A portable plastic record player from the '70s. A handful of fleas. WD-40, for cleaning rubber. 5 boxes of tissues. A collection of dried shit, hidden under a bed.

Latrines

Your dark straight hair a silk skin I wanted to stick my fist through. That Neil Diamond song we practiced all year in the 8th grade out on the front lawn. The album playing in your bedroom. Singing it to each other in the bathroom stalls. How you cried under the redwoods in the national park, worried the raccoons would bite your toes if you slept. How your sleeping bag swarmed with red spiders in the morning. I wanted to show you how to masturbate: I had read about it in my Mother's medical textbook. I wouldn't let you share my sleeping bag, I wouldn't let you borrow my bikini. How you told me not to tell anyone else. I'm not the pig you think I am. I'm not the dog you think I am. I'm not the person you think you are. Can we try this again?

Black Velour

You can't sleep without him in the room, but he doesn't want you in his bed. You sleep under his footboard, arrange his books so they make a comfortable platform. You can sleep an hour at a time this way. You get up around 2 AM and wander the streets; you think no one can tell you're a girl because you wear a knit hat and a puffy down coat. You stare into the windows of other people who can't sleep. You watch a man drag a child down the sidewalk. *But I don't wanna*, the child says, trying to pull his sleeve free—*It's okay*, the man says, a baseball cap covering his eyes. Their voices disappear into the park and you realize that this may be the dream where you're invisible.

Transport

Many years ago, the Gorilla learned how to drive. He likes to drive your brother back and forth to the soccer field. You are never quite certain what happens in the car, but your brother's cheeks start to grow darker, his eyes both larger and hooded.

What Happens When You Try to Write

Your horse is eating your head. He started off with your hair. You guess you can understand that, since your hair is blond and dry in the summer, so it probably looks like hay. You wouldn't think that horses could bite so hard, as they normally munch on grass, but their teeth are enormous—not very sharp, but quite hard. The horse jaw can exert pressures of up to 2,000 pounds per square inch. You made that up. Horse teeth, also, are the size of dominos, and look like thick brown curved dominos, but hurt more than dominos ever could, even if they were thrown quite hard from a near distance. Horses' teeth grow indefinitely and have to be filed down with a large metal file. This process is called "floating." You did not make this up. Also, you grind your own teeth at night. Sometimes you wake up with tiny bits of teeth on your tongue. They don't taste like anything—you spit them out in the sink. Every time you meet a dentist, he becomes very depressed. He often starts to tell you about the country where he came from, how he misses the weather. He inevitably avoids looking in your mouth. He opens your jaws with those rubbery gloved hands, then stares out the window, shaking his head and sighing theatrically. You were surprised when your horse tore off your ear, but since then you haven't felt many emotions. From where you lie on the floor of his stall, you can hear his noisy chewing and crunching, and watch his hind hooves shuffle and tip. Sometimes he swats at a fly with his tail. You find the swish of his tail comforting, regular. It sounds a little like a broom, as if someone were sweeping the stall next to you.

The Animal Gift

Your cat drags a movie star onto your feet while you're sleeping. Under the covers, on top of your feet! The movie star is wet and still. Your first thought, *octopus under my toes,* then you wake up shrieking. The cat shrieks in response and plummets into a wall. When you turn on the lights, you can't see the movie star; she's under the covers. So you make that quick *ugh, ugh* sound you make when you don't know what something is, but you're sure it's disgusting. You stand by the door and rip back the covers. The movie star lies there, curled up, covered in cream suede and cat snot. *Oh Christ!* you yell at the cat, *What the hell is wrong with you.* You see your window's open and slam it shut; that's probably how the movie star got in. You go to the kitchen, cursing at the cat, to get some rubber gloves so you can haul the movie star from your bed. The cat jumps up on the sink and offers you his cheek to kiss—he thinks if he pretends, you can both get beyond this.

The Gorilla's Equipment

A box with a surprise. Something like a hotdog with a vein in it, peeking everywhere you don't look. Lockless doors. A voice like a sped-up fog horn. A miniature woman who hides on the roof and covers her ears.

Latrines

How you were better than me at math, how your painted horses always had an alien gleam. Your hairspray made me sneeze. The song had the word blue over and over. *Do you really think you're an animal?* one boy asked before he hit you on the back of the head, made you fall to the lawn. You apologized for running over my yellow lab with your bike; I never said anything about pissing on your toothbrush. We sat cross-legged on the front lawn, chewing grass blades, the fat, white, tender part. I was sorry your parents pretended to love you. I poured all your change down the latrine. Then I kissed your sleeping hand and, for hours, waved the swarming summer bees away from your face. How I bit your arm once, right after a mosquito, to see what it would taste like. Let me tell you about that summer camp.

The Gorilla on Medication

At ten, you have chronic insomnia, which results in white-out migraines. Your pediatrician prescribes large blue pills of codeine to help you sleep, but the Gorilla won't let you take them. The Gorilla tells you that you're weak, that you should just close your eyes and concentrate to sleep. The Gorilla takes the blue pills and spreads them all over his large rubber palms, then slams them down his throat. He passes out in the paisley La-Z-Boy by the fireplace. The Gorilla drools as he snores.

Black Velour

You can only sleep if this one boy is in the room with you. When you have a fever, you ask him to sit in your room and watch you—the sun a painful yellow peeking around the edges of everything. You have the same dream you had when your Mother used to watch you, wiping a tepid washcloth across your forehead: you're in a room with all the lights on, bowls of blueberries tucked under your feet. Someone angry is pounding at your bedroom door, someone is trying to get in. *Okay,* the door yells. *Okay, okay.* The door is orange, a large rubbery orange. When you wake up, the boy is gone, the blinds pulled back, and the sun unmoving, burning your hands as it touches.

The Gorilla and the Baby

The Gorilla loves babies, but they often cry at the sight of him or at the first whiff of his putrid, yellow breath.

Fake Fur

It is not winter, or it is winter, but not very cold. The sun is missing from the sky; everything is a swirled elephant/ donkey gray. You are holding a sleeping cat on a park bench. The cat's head droops over your arm as if he has no muscles, or is made of rubber. Somewhere in a tree, a gull makes a sound like a small garbage disposal.

How to Make a Red Coat

Take from the lint trap in the dryer all the soft fuzz and thread, and drape it over the faucet in your neighbor's bathtub. Your neighbor won't mind; he misses the horses in his home country and is drunk by breakfast. He sits by the window, refusing to look up or out when you walk in. He's worn the same black pants for days. The smell makes your eyes water, so leave the front door open. Go down to the tiny store under the stairs and buy two gallons of cranberry juice from the depressed pregnant woman. A monster covered in brown feathers will follow you home. He refuses to make a sound, just blinks his large yellow eyes, even when you pluck a feather and slide it into the bucket under your arm. Take the monster by the shoulder and tuck him into your neighbor's bed. Now, during the night, they'll both have a reason to howl.

Gorilla

When you see him out of the corner of your eye, the Gorilla is squatting and pumping with urgency. *Fap!* he goes. *Fap! Fap! Fap!*

The Gorilla finds this funny, all this suffering on account of him. Sometimes he talks in the voice of Arnold Schwarzenegger in that movie, when Schwarzenegger is about to drop a man over a cliff.

Black Velour

You find another boy's couch to sleep on; his roommates don't mind, or they mind only a little. The couch is covered in flaking black velour—you can hear trucks loading and unloading outside. When you tuck your hands under your arms, you are warm enough. You pretend you are deep in the ocean, asleep, or asleep on an airplane, your forehead tipped on a hard cold oval that looks out on a space moving slowly, something gray.

Shadow

The Gorilla is frightened by his shadow—when he sees it creep beneath him on the street, he yelps and quivers. He then proceeds to go home and kick his dog. His dog is small, and so elderly that most of its teeth have slipped away. It needs to be fed oatmeal and ground chuck by hand. When the Gorilla beats the dog, it doesn't cry or bark; it simply curls into itself, smaller and smaller, whining like a tiny balloon.

The Watcher on the 6th Floor

Melissa says you have to stand outside the bathroom stall with the door open, sometimes you have to hold the door open, pressing high up on the chipped pink metal, because they often swing closed on their own. Some of the stalls have strips of torn fabric or pieces of clothesline to fasten around the corner of the door and keep it open. Then you try not to look at their faces and just watch what they're doing with their hands, make sure they're not pouring in anything from their pockets or underwear. Usually you don't have to talk. Sometimes they'll say something, but you don't have to respond.

Driving

The Gorilla teaches you how to drive. He does this mostly by bellowing from the driver's seat and shoving his hand between your thighs. When you're alone, you start crashing. You flatten a stop sign, a small cyclist, the back wall of the garage. The Gorilla finds this funny, funny until the insurance goes up.

The Smell of Wet Fur

Sunburn. The lake. A woman with short brown curly hair (you can't see her face) lifts up her bikini strap. On her shoulder, her skin is brick red and then in the space under the strap, half-shadowed, white. The furiously green trees in the background have extra crisp edges—no distance blur. You can hear splashing and the sound of a beach ball being whacked. Somebody's laughing; somebody's speaking quietly.

Shallow river. Unnaturally blue, flowing down a hillside into mud. It's raining lightly and ruining the carnival. You have stolen something and hid it under a bench. The organizer comes to find you and you try to look innocent. You deserve this thing, this small thing that fits in your two hands. No one else needs it as much as you. You wish the performance was over already.

Transport II

The Gorilla rides the subway with you. You find the ugliest woman on the train and point: *See that? That's what I feel like right now.* The woman pretends not to notice.

How to Survive a Sinking Ship

Wave hands, palm outwards, in a slow and graceful motion. Warm sweaters. A history of movies ending with a sunset. A tendency to avoid artichoke hearts. Run up and down near the railing, get your circulation going—you will need it! Tie heavy objects around your neck. Put your last will and testament in the toes of your tap shoes. Practice "glug-glug" to yourself. Say it in a whisper. Pucker your mouth so you look like a goldfish. Jump into the arms of the nearest captain. A sore back. Abrupt seating on deck. Water the color of tarnished coins, of old shoes. It is only true if you say it is. Water can be both heavy and cold. The swimming pool is so uninviting; deck chairs like fallen tentacles. Ignore the moans of the elderly, take their hats and see how far they sail. All along, you were only entertainment. The stage has shifted left, then down.

Gorilla Autopsy

You have held a heart close to your nose. It smelled of cold and fungicide. So tough, your scalpel slipped instead of slicing: you screamed like a girl in disgust and frustration. Inside it had holes and more rot. It was slippery, heavy—you became dizzy. You saw the toads splayed and skinned, pinned to the wall, beckoning to you, the red pin heads bobbing. You wiped your palms on your blouse, your backpack, the paper towels. Your lab partner refused to look at you, spent the whole class in the corner with his girlfriend, trying to wend his fingers through the slit in her stone-washed skirt.

The Future

Yesterday, your dead cat Tinkerbell visited you in the bathroom and described a plane ride in your future. According to Tinkerbell, the plane will stop and hover, making sounds like a little boy being a helicopter. You are not to worry. You will land some place warm where plants grow out of building cornices and the plants.

You were too busy trying to feed the ghost of your brother to hear the whole thing—he was demanding eggs, and the rotten ham sandwich you had buried at the bottom of the garbage. Your brother was so hungry, but he couldn't quite get the food to his mouth. His hands were broken or absent, he was trying to tell you.

Large Rubber Claws

The Gorilla is pounding the back of your brother's head against the side of the garage. Your brother's head makes a small thud as it hits, like an impatiently tapping boot. Your brother's mouth is making a loud noise. The sun moves in patches over the Gorilla's fur, over the driveway—the soap bubbles underneath the newly washed car glisten and hide.

Black Velour

After three days with no sleep, you meet some new boys. You are constantly weeping, your teeth chattering. One of the boys suggests warm milk, the other pets your hair and tells you he's busy. They are angry that you can't remember their names.

Becoming Your Mother

Find out where the history happened; wear her hat, her shoes. Go to her crash site—forage for shards. Secretly unlock the gate and herd all the horses onto the freeway with your motorcycle—act horrified when one gets hit by a pick-up. Pick up the gin bottle with her fingerprints on it; pretend to have TB. Pretend to be promiscuous. Pretend men mean nothing to you. It's best to let these diseases take their course. Tilt the brim of your cloche. Take a course in beekeeping so you can say the word "honey" with complete sincerity. Practice your feminine cough. Practice eating by swallowing everything. Weakly, ask the men to gather round your bedside. Hand each one a packet of smeared envelopes; pretend the letters inside aren't blank.

Gorilla Suit

A woman is trying to get you off her lawn. Her black beehive wig towers over you, a hostile ice cream cone. She tries shutting the gate, but you are already on the inside. *We don't want your kind here*, she hisses.

I have a message for your daughter, you say, warding off the blows of her pocketbook, your hands bloody. In the top story window, a hairless girl watches you. She chews slowly on the lace curtain. *I don't have a daughter*, the woman shouts again. You know the girl is watching you, waiting to see what you'll crush next.

Learning to Swim on Dry Land

Sink: Let the water fill your hair, your ears. Don't worry about your breath, it will take care of itself. Keep busy—there is always more to do in the kitchen. Polish the spoons! Burn the toast! It is good to wreck things so you can start over. In this way, you may regain your youth. Take your miniature tea set out of storage and tie each piece to a branch in your backyard's oak—the blue jays will have something to fight for. Avoid the roof; don't stare at the sky for too long. Blue as a newborn's skull—it will pierce you, if you let it. Pretend to shadow box with your neighbor. Pretend to have a neighbor. Develop a taste for bad French tarts—hide the smeared boxes under the front porch. Clap, clap twice! Your schnauzer will whine and spin on her hind legs, dancing like a petite ballerina who is both blind and ugly. Draw a mustache under her nose with the ashes of your money. Expect gladiolus to bloom in that pile of trash by the chain link fence, just because you spit there twice. Now try to breathe and flail your arms; find out if the Gorilla is watching.

The Gorilla in Swimtrunks

The Gorilla decides you and he will take the subway to the beach. You start to take the A train to Far Rockaway, but there's construction at 59th Street, so you switch to the D to Coney Island. Just as you're entering Brooklyn, the train stops in the tunnel. Lights flick on and off. The Gorilla gets restless, shits his pants. People move away in concentric circles of dismay. The train hums, shudders and goes still.

The conductor gets on the loudspeaker, asks Ralph to give him a hand. No one moves but the Gorilla. He grabs a pole, sways back and forth, his wet trunks hanging low.

Ralph does not appear. The conductor asks for him again, repeats himself twice, sounds angry. You all look for Ralph. No one admits to it. The air conditioner starts, then goes silent. The Gorilla sits on the floor.

People try to pry open the doors, using fingernails, umbrellas. In their efforts, they shout and laugh. No one can open a door. The men and women become quiet again and look at the floor. A man in the back plays with the ringtones on his cell. The conductor calls for Ralph. The Gorilla complains that the beach is always this way. You say, *No, sometimes it rains.*

Your Dead Labrador Retriever Visits in the Form of a Hostess

Then, around eight that morning, you saw the big woman in your garden. She lay between the mounds of snow in a red cocktail dress, her shoulders exposed, the thin straps of her dress biting into her fat white shoulders. You couldn't see her face; she was lying with her back to the window, using her arm as a pillow. She wore scuffed, high-heeled silver sandals—her legs crossed at the ankles. You stuck your forehead against the glass, hoping to see more. The glass was cold and comfortable against your skin, but after half an hour, your head started to ache. The ache had a beat, in/out. You breathed against the glass and drew an outline of the woman in the steam. You put on slippers, and then your large, tan, puffy coat, still stained from last week's dog puke. The woman didn't move when you squatted and poked her with a hanger. You touched her shoulder and she felt hot, like frying pan hot. She sighed and rolled over, and said, without opening her eyes, *Never mind. I was just trying to see if the door was really alarmed.*

First Date

The Gorilla is telling you not to go too far on your first date. He demonstrates what "too far" is with your Mother. You worry the neighbors might hear. He tells you, his breath rasping behind the rubber lips, "Why buy the milk, when you can get the cow for free?" That phrase plants itself under your toenails, in the conch shell part of your inner ear.

You start to hear, "Why fry the monk, when you can eat the nun for free?" On Tuesday it becomes, "Sigh, she said milk!, and you got only fat-free?" After, it hums constantly in the background: "Shy women are meek, let you only watch TV?" *Eyes on me now, or you'll feel like a dying bee?* "Cry on, bald guy, your tears are strictly rated G?" *Since you've been home, I feel so greatly off key?* "My tailor said silk, and you left this sow for me?" *Thumbelina, Thumbelina, leap off that burning tree!*

What If (Sci-Fi Version)

What happens if the blue test tube cracks in your fist? Will you wear a red skirt under your lab smock? Will the white coats run after you barefoot? Will your glasses fall or will they dangle from one ear? Have you lost track of the Gorilla and then, how many languages will you swear in? Will the explosion fling you to the ceiling, and will you find the violet crystal there?

Will you lose your eyelashes in the bright tumble of the Bunsen burner or just set the lab on fire? Will the voodoo doll ever be discovered behind the table of the elements? Will the radioactive grass overcome the runners after? The lab notes say: You recognize the complex equations written in chalk across your back. Your braids will loosen as the skirt's hem unravels. With a drop of blood and some chemicals, you might understand the escape route, the chart of red arrows, taped to the back of the cloak room door—

About the Author

Christine Hamm spent twelve years helping to house homeless women in New York City before she became an English professor. She has published four full-length collections of poetry exploring the roles of animals, fairytales, gender, and violence. Her PhD in English was an ecocritical look at the poetry of Marianne Moore, Elizabeth Bishop, and Sylvia Plath. Her poems have been published in *Painted Bride Quarterly*, *Rattle*, *Rhino*, *Nat Brut*, *Pinch*, and *American Chordata*. She also has an MSW from NYU, an MA in fiction writing, and is half-way through an MFA in poetry from Columbia. She lives in New Jersey with her husband and many pets, and teaches at Seton Hall.

About The Word Works

Since its founding in 1974, The Word Works has steadily published volumes of contemporary poetry and presented public programs. Its imprints include The Washington Prize, The Tenth Gate Prize, The Hilary Tham Capital Collection, and International Editions.

Monthly, The Word Works offers free literary programs in the Chevy Chase, MD, Café Muse series, and each summer it holds free poetry programs in Washington, D. C.'s Rock Creek Park. Word Works programs have included "In the Shadow of the Capitol," a symposium and archival project on the African American intellectual community in segregated Washington, D.C.; the Gunston Arts Center Poetry Series; the Poet Editor panel discussions at The Writer's Center; Master Class workshops; and a writing retreat in Tuscany, Italy.

As a 501(c)3 organization, The Word Works has received awards from the National Endowment for the Arts, the National Endowment for the Humanities, the D.C. Commission on the Arts & Humanities, the Witter Bynner Foundation, Poets & Writers, The Writer's Center, Bell Atlantic, the David G. Taft Foundation, and others, including many generous private patrons.

An archive of artistic and administrative materials in the Washington Writing Archive housed in the George Washington University Gelman Library. It is a member of the Community of Literary Magazines and Presses and its books are distributed by Small Press Distribution.

wordworksbooks.org

THE TENTH GATE PRIZE

Jennifer Barber, *Works on Paper*, 2015
Christine Hamm, *Gorilla*, 2019
Lisa Lewis, *Taxonomy of the Missing*, 2017
Brad Richard, *Parasite Kingdom*, 2018
Roger Sedarat, *Haji As Puppet*, 2016
Lisa Sewell, *Impossible Object*, 2014

INTERNATIONAL EDITIONS

Kajal Ahmad (Alana Marie Levinson-LaBrosse, Mewan
      Nahro Said Sofi, and Darya Abdul-Karim Ali Najin,
      trans., with Barbara Goldberg), *Handful of Salt*
Keyne Cheshire (trans.), *Murder at Jagged Rock: A Tragedy by Sophocles*
Jeannette L. Clariond (Curtis Bauer, trans.), *Image of Absence*
Jean Cocteau (Mary-Sherman Willis, trans.), *Grace Notes*
Yoko Danno & James C. Hopkins, *The Blue Door*
Moshe Dor (Barbara Goldberg, trans.), *Scorched by the Sun*
Moshe Dor, Barbara Goldberg, Giora Leshem, eds.,
      The Stones Remember: Native Israeli Poets
Laura Cesarco Eglin (Jesse Lee Kercheval and Catherine Jagoe,
trans.), *Reborn in Ink*
Vladimir Levchev (Henry Taylor, trans.), *Black Book of the
      Endangered Species*
Lee Sang (Myong-Hee Kim, trans.) *Crow's Eye View: The Infamy
      of Lee Sang, Korean Poet*

THE HILARY THAM CAPITAL COLLECTION

Nathalie Anderson, *Stain*
Mel Belin, *Flesh That Was Chrysalis*
Carrie Bennett, *The Land Is a Painted Thing*
Doris Brody, *Judging the Distance*
Sarah Browning, *Whiskey in the Garden of Eden*
Grace Cavalieri, *Pinecrest Rest Haven*
Cheryl Clarke, *By My Precise Haircut*
Christopher Conlon, *Gilbert and Garbo in Love*
        & *Mary Falls: Requiem for Mrs. Surratt*
Donna Denizé, *Broken Like Job*
W. Perry Epes, *Nothing Happened*
David Eye, *Seed*
Bernadette Geyer, *The Scabbard of Her Throat*
Elizabeth Gross, *this body / that lightning show*
Barbara G. S. Hagerty, *Twinzilla*
Lisa Hase-Jackson, *Flint & Fire*
James Hopkins, *Eight Pale Women*
Donald Illich, *Chance Bodies*
Brandon Johnson, *Love's Skin*
Thomas March, *Aftermath*
Marilyn McCabe, *Perpetual Motion*
Judith McCombs, *The Habit of Fire*
James McEwen, *Snake Country*
Miles David Moore, *The Bears of Paris* & *Rollercoaster*
Kathi Morrison-Taylor, *By the Nest*
Tera Vale Ragan, *Reading the Ground*
Michael Shaffner, *The Good Opinion of Squirrels*
Maria Terrone, *The Bodies We Were Loaned*
Hilary Tham, *Bad Names for Women* & *Counting*
Barbara Ungar, *Charlotte Brontë, You Ruined My Life*
        & *Immortal Medusa*
Jonathan Vaile, *Blue Cowboy*
Rosemary Winslow, *Green Bodies*
Kathleen Winter, *Transformer*
Michele Wolf, *Immersion*
Joe Zealberg, *Covalence*

THE WASHINGTON PRIZE

Nathalie Anderson, *Following Fred Astaire*, 1998

Michael Atkinson, *One Hundred Children Waiting for a Train*, 2001

Molly Bashaw, *The Whole Field Still Moving Inside It*, 2013

Carrie Bennett, *biography of water*, 2004

Peter Blair, *Last Heat*, 1999

John Bradley, *Love-in-Idleness: The Poetry of Roberto Zingarello*, 1995, 2ND edition 2014

Christopher Bursk, *The Way Water Rubs Stone*, 1988

Richard Carr, *Ace*, 2008

Jamison Crabtree, *Rel[AM]ent*, 2014

Jessica Cuello, *Hunt*, 2016

Barbara Duffey, *Simple Machines*, 2015

B. K. Fischer, *St. Rage's Vault*, 2012

Linda Lee Harper, *Toward Desire*, 1995

Ann Rae Jonas, *A Diamond Is Hard But Not Tough*, 1997

Susan Lewis, *Zoom*, 2017

Frannie Lindsay, *Mayweed*, 2009

Richard Lyons, *Fleur Carnivore*, 2005

Elaine Magarrell, *Blameless Lives*, 1991

Fred Marchant, *Tipping Point*, 1993, 2ND edition 2013

Nils Michals, *Gembox*, 2018

Ron Mohring, *Survivable World*, 2003

Barbara Moore, *Farewell to the Body*, 1990

Brad Richard, *Motion Studies*, 2010

Jay Rogoff, *The Cutoff*, 1994

Prartho Sereno, *Call from Paris*, 2007, 2ND edition 2013

Enid Shomer, *Stalking the Florida Panther*, 1987

John Surowiecki, *The Hat City After Men Stopped Wearing Hats*, 2006

Miles Waggener, *Phoenix Suites*, 2002

Charlotte Warren, *Gandhi's Lap*, 2000

Mike White, *How to Make a Bird with Two Hands*, 2011

Nancy White, *Sun, Moon, Salt*, 1992, 2ND edition 2010

George Young, *Spinoza's Mouse*, 1996

OTHER WORD WORKS BOOKS

Annik Adey-Babinski, *Okay Cool No Smoking Love Pony*
Karren L. Alenier, *Wandering on the Outside*
Karren L. Alenier, ed., *Whose Woods These Are*
Karren L. Alenier & Miles David Moore, eds.,
    Winners: A Retrospective of the Washington Prize
Christopher Bursk, ed., *Cool Fire*
Willa Carroll, *Nerve Chorus*
Grace Cavalieri, *Creature Comforts*
Abby Chew, *A Bear Approaches from the Sky*
Nadia Colburn, *The High Shelf*
Henry Crawford, *The Binary Planet*
Barbara Goldberg, *Berta Broadfoot and Pepin the Short*
Akua Lezli Hope, *Them Gone*
Frannie Lindsay, *If Mercy*
Elaine Maggarrell, *The Madness of Chefs*
Marilyn McCabe, *Glass Factory*
Kevin McLellan, *Ornitheology*
JoAnne McFarland, *Identifying the Body*
Leslie McGrath, *Feminists Are Passing from Our Lives*
Ann Pelletier, *Letter That Never*
Ayaz Pirani, *Happy You Are Here*
W.T. Pfefferle, *My Coolest Shirt*
Jacklyn Potter, Dwaine Rieves, Gary Stein, eds.,
    Cabin Fever: Poets at Joaquin Miller's Cabin
Robert Sargent, *Aspects of a Southern Story*
    & *A Woman from Memphis*
Julia Story, *Spinster for Hire*
Miles Waggener, *Superstition Freeway*
Fritz Ward, *Tsunami Diorama*
Camille-Yvette Welsh, *The Four Ugliest Children in Christendom*
Amber West, *Hen & God*
Maceo Whitaker, *Narco Farm*
Nancy White, ed., *Word for Word*